FUNdamental Soccer

Written by **Karl Dewazien**

This book is dedicated to **Vincent** and **Wadja Dewazien,** the individuals who made me possible!

Karl Dewazien

FUNdamental Soccer

Written by **Karl Dewazien**
United States Soccer Federation "A" Licensed Coach

I will use "HE", in this book, generically to refer to both boys and girls for the sake of brevity.

ISBN 0-9619139-3-2

Printed by **Fresno Envelope** • Fresno, California
Book Design by **Keith Bennett** • Valley Type & Design
Illustrations • **Joseph G. Garcia**
Editors • **Terri Monson** and **Vincent J. Lavery**

FUN Soccer Enterprises
828 E. Portland Ave.
Fresno, CA. 93720
www.fundamentalsoccer.com

Soccer is a simple game to understand. It is a contest between two teams of equal numbers. Once a team has control of the ball. All the players become part of the Attacking team. Their aim is to control, pass, dribble and shoot the ball across the opponents goal line, underneath the crossbar and between the goal posts for a score. Should the team lose possession of the ball, an immediate transition takes place, and all players become part of the Defending team. Their aim is to make every effort to regain ball possession and prevent the opponent from scoring. The main objective of the game is to score more goals than your opponent.

Soccer is a simple game to play. It requires the simple skills of control, dribble, pass and shooting the ball. What makes great soccer players is perfecting these simple skills.

Soccer is a simple game to coach. Requiring simple skills of reading, studying and understanding the information presented in the "FUNdamental SOCCER" Book & DVD Series. What will make you a successful youth soccer coach is the patient application of this information.

FUNdamental Soccer

Section 1

Get to Know Your Players

Learning Steps

Coaching Steps

Before holding your first practice session you should...
Get To Know Your Players.

Make a conscious effort to get to know each player on a personal basis.

Talk about mutual goals both short and long term.

Make all conversation "two-way".

During these talks it is very important to find out...
If the player is really interested in playing soccer?

Find out each individual's playing background:

Number of years involved?

Favorite coach & why?

Favorite positions?

Personal strengths and weaknesses?

Note: It is an irrefutable fact that knowing some Child Psychology can help you deal better with the age group you are working with.

Generally speaking:

The decision to play soccer in the
U-10 age group is influenced by
Parents.

The decision to play soccer in the
U-14 age group is influenced by
Peers.

In both instances you will be faced with players who are not interested in playing soccer and adjustments must be made accordingly.

Give appropriate attention to the disinterested player
but not at   the expense of the rest of the team.

Make the practices so much FUN that the disinterested
player will want to join!

Know How Your Players Learn

Observing
By watching the coach, advanced players, videos or film on the technique they are to perform.

Feeling
By touching the part of the foot or body which will be involved when they perform the technique.

Hearing
By listening "carefully" to instructions when they are given.

Visualizing / Imagery
By seeing themselves performing the technique.

Imitating
By re-enacting the technique observed.

Self-Talking
By repeating the "buzz words" while they are imitating.

Practicing*
By repeating the proper use of the technique, and correcting mistakes in the process until it's perfected and becomes a Habit.

Testing
By playing against others, checking progress first in practice, at home, finally in an actual game.

Try to make practice error free.

STEP 1 - Explanation

Communicate in simple everyday language.

Create or use *"buzz words"* (Words that "trigger" the mind to highlight points of emphasis)

For Example

Dribbling..."Push...Stop...Step"

Helpful Hints:

Take into consideration the attention span of your players and adjust the length of your explanation accordingly...Be brief!

After you have dealt with a point...ask questions to make sure the point was understood; repeat the verbal instructions only if necessary...Be brief!

I Hear and I Forget

Be brief!

STEP 2 - Demostration

*Give a **demonstration** – Slowly, Simply and technically correct.*

Make it completely clear what points the demonstration is intended to bring out.

Important: If you are unable to demonstrate, then have a guest instructor or one of your better players do the demonstration for you!

While the demonstration is taking place make sure that everything can be seen clearly by all players.

I See and I Remember – Slow, Correct and Brief!

STEP 3 - Touching

As the demonstration and explanation are taking place...

*Have the players make contact with (**touch**) the part of the shoe or body which will come into play when they perform the technique.*

Important:
This helps in programming the brain and muscles to work together.

STEP 3 - Visualizing

After the demonstration/explanation and touching.

Have the players close their eyes and imagine themselves performing the technique correctly and proficiently.

Important: This powerful method is currently being used by many international athletes who realize that the body can better achieve what the mind has rehearsed.

STEP 5 - Self-Talk

As they are "visualizing"

*Have the players repeat the "buzz words" **out-loud!***

PUSH! STOP! STEP!

This will let you know if: They listened to your instructions. They are indeed visualizing or just resting their eyes.

STEP 6 - Action

After using the previously mentioned confidence building tools.

Perform the technique using the – ***Stages of Play:***
   First work with/against a ***walking*** partner.
   Then work with/against a ***jogging*** partner.
   Finally work with/against a partner playing at ***game speed.***

Partner increases pressure as confidence and ability increase.

I Do and I Understand.
Activity, good repetition, experimentation and enjoyment lead to success!

STEP 7 - Observe

As the players experiment with performing the technique...

Look for weaknesses in the execution of the movement/technique.

Very Important: *Discipline your mind* to focus only on what is being taught and *ignoring all other mistakes.*

Avoid causing Paralysis through Analysis.

STEP 8 - Correct

Consistent basic faults can be corrected by:

Asking a guided question: "Which part of the shoe…?"

Using the 'sandwich approach': Begin with a positive statement. Follow with point of refinement and end with a positive statement!

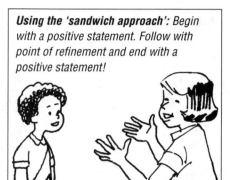

Reverse coaching - Have the player teach you!

Repetition of movement - Have the player do the action very slowly!

Kinesiology - Physically adjust the player's body to help him achieve the correct form through a realization of how it "feels".

Helpful Hints: When in doubt, **Go back to basics.** Break down the skill to its component parts.

Very Important:
In all cases restart with the correct move or maneuver.

STEP 9 - Test

Perform the technique against opposition:

| First: ONE vs. ONE game. | Then: SMALL SIDED game. | Finally: SCRIMMAGE or OFFICIAL game. |

Helpful Hint: Be careful that in the haste of competing the technique does not deteriorate.

STEP 10 - Confirm

Critique to see what learning has taken place!

Helpful Hint: Do not expect to see in a game anything that was not accomplished in practice.

Throughout This Ten Step Coaching Sequence:

Be patient! *You must not expect immediate results*

Be persistent! *It will take time and effective repetition.*

Be flexible! *So that you can maintain players' interest when working on a particular soccer technique.*

Maintain that sense of humor! *The players should work in a relaxed atmosphere.*

Reward! *With a positive reaction, a positive comment or smile.*

Remember, Everything Takes Time To Learn!

Visit our website:
FUNdamentalsoccer.com
for exchanging great ideas!

FUNdamental Soccer

Soccer

Section 2

Planning Considerations

You Will Need Players

TEAMMATES - *For realism establish familiarity.*

OPPONENTS - *For realism force decision making.*

Consider

Number at practice

Age

Interests

Needs

You Will Need Players

Work with the ball to:
Develop soccer technique, build ball control and confidence.

Large field of play to:
Keep the ball in continuous play.
Provide more space in which to perform .
Create more opportunities to recover after making a mistake.

Fewer opposing players to:
Assure an increased number of touches with the ball.
Create more opportunities to succeed against opposition.

As players become more proficient in using the basic techniques of the game against opposition, plan and act accordingly!

You Will Need Safe Facilities

ONE + ONE - and - ONE vs. ONE FIELD(s)

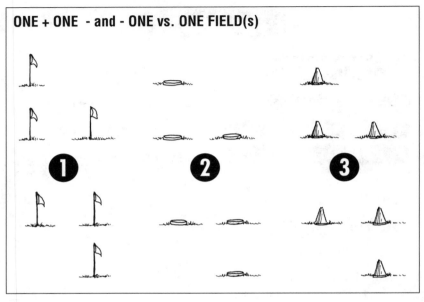

SMALL SIDED GAME FIELD(s): Checkerboard system.

Checkerboard System

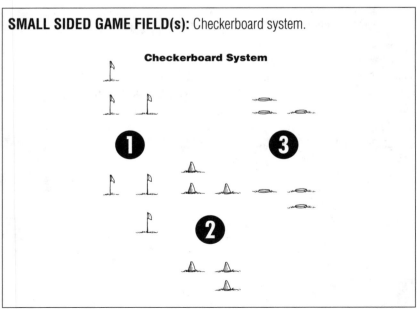

You Will Need Safe Facilities

Fields with-in the Field: Section the field to achieve maximum learning.

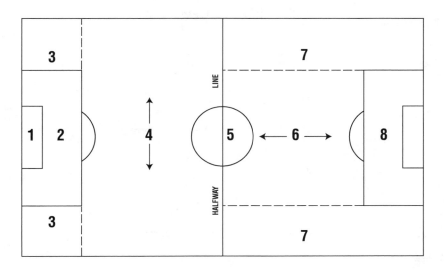

The Formula: Number of Players on Larger Team (x) 10 yards = Length of Field

Some examples:

Even sided games.

1 vs. 1	Length = 10 yards
2 vs. 2	Length = 20 yards
5 vs. 5	Length = 50 yards
8 vs. 8	Length = 80 yards
11 vs. 11	Length = 110 yards

Uneven sides games.

1 vs. 0	Length = 10 yards
2 vs. 1	Length = 20 yards
5 vs. 3	Length = 50 yards
8 vs. 5	Length = 80 yards
11 vs. 7	Length = 110 yards

Note: Your use of cones, flags and other markers becomes extremely important if you do not have the luxury of being able to use marked fields.

You Will Need Two Goals

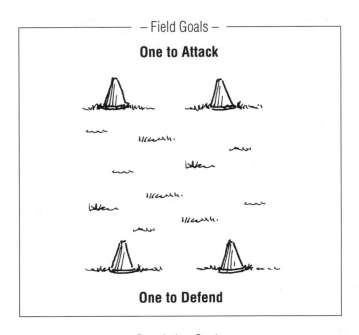

– Field Goals –

One to Attack

One to Defend

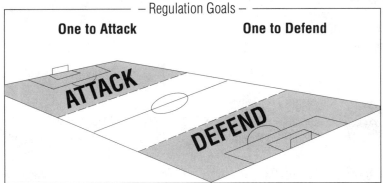

– Regulation Goals –

One to Attack   **One to Defend**

ATTACK

DEFEND

Note: Your use of cones, flags and other markers becomes extremely important if you do not have the luxury of being able to use regulation goals. Check with administration for official size of regulation goal used in your age group.

You Will Need Two Goals

Vital: All practice games must include two goals:

Players must learn to instinctively respond by **reading** ball possession. This means:

Their ball = "read" = defend.

Our ball = "read" = attack.

Good habits are created in a *good practice environment.*

– Good habits are timesavers because they allow players to "Attack and Defend" without having to stop and think.

– Two dimensional players, ones who can attack and defend, are developed in this habit forming environment.

You Will Need Equipment

Coach's Responsibility (Team Manager)

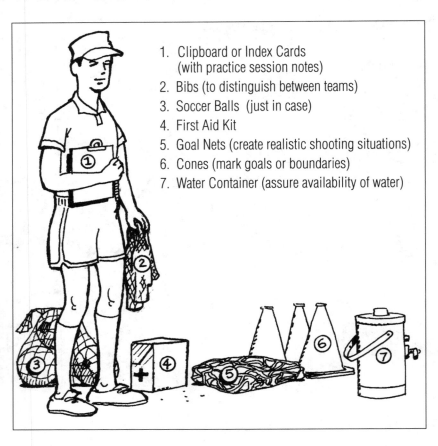

1. Clipboard or Index Cards
   (with practice session notes)
2. Bibs (to distinguish between teams)
3. Soccer Balls (just in case)
4. First Aid Kit
5. Goal Nets (create realistic shooting situations)
6. Cones (mark goals or boundaries)
7. Water Container (assure availability of water)

Optional items:

Air Pump & Needle (properly inflate balls)
Whistle (game control and assembly)
Pen and Note Pad (jot down important notes for future review)
Watch (stop and start on time)
Stopwatch (to time improvement & events)
Marking Pen (for identification marking player/team articles)
Magnetic Playing Field (to use as visual aid)
Tape Recorder (music for warm-up and crowd noise during practice)

You Will Need Equipment Player's Responsibility (Parent)

Sweatsuit

Individual Water Bottle

Shinguards
(mandatory, to be worn at all games & practices)

Socks
(second pair)

Soccer ball
(mandatory and initialed)

Shoes
(mandatory, same pair to be used during league game)

Shoelaces
(extra pair)

You Will Need a Timetable

Your FUNdamental Practice Routine truly establishes each practice as a
Rehearsal for Game Day!

SAMPLE TIMETABLE

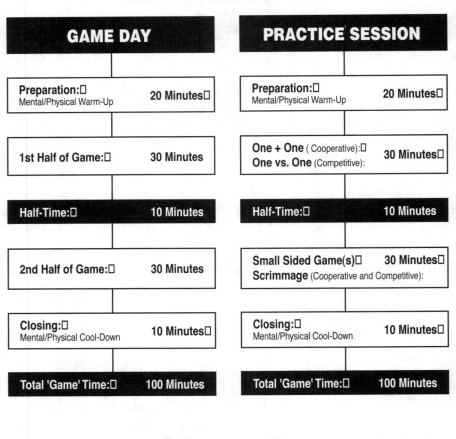

GAME DAY		PRACTICE SESSION	
Preparation: Mental/Physical Warm-Up	20 Minutes	**Preparation:** Mental/Physical Warm-Up	20 Minutes
1st Half of Game:	30 Minutes	**One + One** (Cooperative): **One vs. One** (Competitive):	30 Minutes
Half-Time:	10 Minutes	**Half-Time:**	10 Minutes
2nd Half of Game:	30 Minutes	**Small Sided Game(s)** **Scrimmage** (Cooperative and Competitive):	30 Minutes
Closing: Mental/Physical Cool-Down	10 Minutes	**Closing:** Mental/Physical Cool-Down	10 Minutes
Total 'Game' Time:	100 Minutes	**Total 'Game' Time:**	100 Minutes

Remember
Practice is Rehearsal for Game Day!

You Will Need to Be Realistic

Ask yourself, **does it happen in the game?**
If the answer is **no, then do not do it in practice!**

*For example, **standing in lines.***

Your Practice Will Not Be:
- Too simple, players will get bored.
- Too complex, players will get confused.

Your Practice Will Be:
- Creative, so that learning will continuously take place.

If you follow the FUNdamental Practice Routine you will:
- Duplicate the excitement of the game in your practice sessions.
- Create an atmosphere where the players are allowed to teach themselves.
- Create an environment which forces the players to make decisions and learn on their own.
- Create an environment that develops instinctive attacking and defending habits.

You will learn to apply the FUNdamental Practice Motto:
The genius of good coaching is to make hard work seem FUN!

Your FUNdamental Practice Routine follows Newton's law of inertia, 'A player at rest will tend to remain at rest and a player in motion will tend to remain in motion.

Minimize listening and lecture time.

Maximize touches with the ball and playing time.

FUNdamental Soccer

Practice

Section 3

Establish a Theme

Establish a Ritual

You Will Need a Theme

Carefully observe your team in action and determine:

Who *is having problems?*

What *is the major problem/weakness?*

*Key on this **one** topic or **theme** to be discussed, developed and improved at the next practice session.*

Helpful Hints:

Take mental and written notes. Great observers avoid being ball watchers, becoming emotionally involved in the action; managing players' actions assessing and assisting the referee!

You Will Need a Theme

Theme(s) for Attack

Read the Game (page 96)
Run to Attack (page 100)
Receive the Ball (page 103)
Retain the Ball (page 110)
Release the Ball (page 119)
Throw-In (page 134)

Theme(s) for Defense

Read the Game (page 138)
Run to Defend (page 140)
Ready Stance (page 142)
Refuse Advancing (page 146)
Regain the Ball (page 150)

Pre-Practice Ritual

- Arriving early.
- Checking weather and field conditions.

Greeting the players and socializing.

Encouraging them to socialize with each other.

Pre-Practice Ritual

Juggle:
- It is a terrific idea to add ball gymnastics...to the pre-practice routine.
- For personal challenge and FUN.
- Feeling for movement and coordination of/with the ball.

Note: Encourage them to 'juggle' every day. In time their ball control problems will go away!

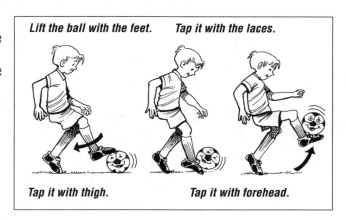

Lift the ball with the feet.   *Tap it with the laces.*

Tap it with thigh.   *Tap it with forehead.*

Play a Fun Game:

Soccer Marbles
Number of players: One vs. One.
Field of play: Open area.
Objective: To hit opponent's ball with your ball.
Rules: Start game with one player passing his ball in any direction.
                     Players alternate, attempt to hit partners ball.
                     Score two points for hitting moving ball.
                     Score one point for hitting stationary ball.

Visit our website:
FUNdamentalsoccer.com
for more Pre-Practice Ritual ideas!

FUNdamental Soccer

Section 4

Nine Step
FUNdamental Practice Routine

THE FLOW

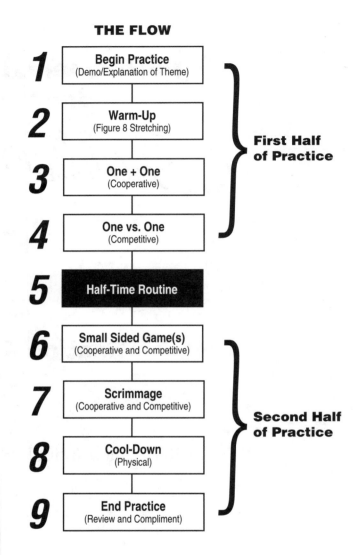

1 Begin Practice
(Demo/Explanation of Theme)

2 Warm-Up
(Figure 8 Stretching)

3 One + One
(Cooperative)

4 One vs. One
(Competitive)

} **First Half of Practice**

5 Half-Time Routine

6 Small Sided Game(s)
(Cooperative and Competitive)

7 Scrimmage
(Cooperative and Competitive)

8 Cool-Down
(Physical)

9 End Practice
(Review and Compliment)

} **Second Half of Practice**

Guarantee:
Patient, consistent-sequential exposure to this FUNdamental practice routine will produce real results.

Teach the Theme

Gather - Bring the players to a defined comfortable area.

Name the theme - Tell the players what they are expected to learn or improve. State clearly the ONE goal to be achieved!

*Give a **demonstration** – Slowly, simply and technically correct.*

Make it completely clear what points the demonstration is intended to bring out.

Remember to use:
- Touching
- Visualizing
- Self talk

Objectives: Preparing players for rigorous practice activities.
Create habit that may prevent injuries in the future.

Preparing players for the rigorous activity of a practice or game is vitally important. Most fitness experts agree that a warm up is essential for optimal performance and injury prevention. The initial stage should consist of light running or jogging to increase the blood supply to the muscles, increase the rate and force of muscle contractions and raise the body and muscle temperature.

Figure 8 Stretch Routine

Number of players: Full team.

Equipment: One ball and two cones (objects) per player.

Marked out square: Size depends on age, skill level, and number of players involved.

Figure 8 Stretch Routine

Sequence:
1. Dribble inside square.
2. Signal, lay out cones (objects).
3. Figure 8.
4. Stretch.
5. Signal, pick up cones (objects).
6. Dribble inside square.
7. Repeat sequence.

Note: Let players make up a 'signal' or 'magic word' (example: 'Cool').
For variety change the 'signal' or 'magic word' at each practice.

Figure 8 Stretch Routine

2. Signal and Laying Out Cones

Objectives: Create appropriate working environment.

Sequence: 1. On 'signal' (cool) players stop ball and put feet together.
2. Hold cones (objects) in outstretched hands.
3. Move right foot as far as possible. Place cone outside of foot.
4. Bring feet back together.
5. Move left foot as far as possible. Place cone outside of foot.

6. Immediately start moving ball in figure eight motion.

Note: Laying out cones can also be used for stretching by holding stretch position for specific number of seconds.

Figure 8 Stretch Routine

3. Controlling the Ball in Figure 8

Objectives: Building confidence by playing the ball with every step or stride.

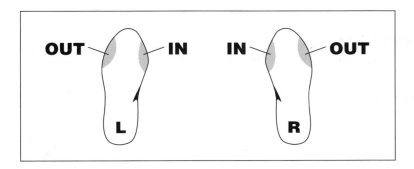

Specific Instructions that can be given:

Left Foot
Outside-Instep (only)
Inside- Instep (only)
Alternate outside-inside with each touch
Player's choice.

Right Foot
Outside-Instep (only)
Inside-Instep (only)
Alternate outside-inside
Player's choice

Alternating

Left foot (touch)   Right foot (touch)
Left outside   Right outside
Left inside   Right inside
Player's choice – ball touches must be with alternating feet.

Notes: Ask for increase of speed as confidence builds. Go from walking (if necessary) to game speed (if possible). Be careful in the haste of increasing speed technique may deteriorate.

Figure 8 Stretch Routine

3. Controlling the Ball in Figure 8

Objectives: To develop ball sensitivity, coordination, flexibility, agility, body control. In short, confidence in keeping possession of the ball.

Dancing Stork

Stationary ball - Place right sole on the ball - then hop on left foot with right returning to ball. (Switch feet)

Move ball in Figure 8 - While hopping on right foot, move the ball right, left, forward and backward using the sole of left foot.

Variation - "Ball contact foot" touches with outer-inner instep.

Kangaroo Dance

Stationary ball - While hopping, alternate foot touches (sole) with the top of the ball.

Move ball in Figure 8 - While hopping, move the ball right, left, forward, and backward while alternating right and left foot touches (sole).

Figure 8 Stretch Routine

3. Controlling the Ball in Figure 8

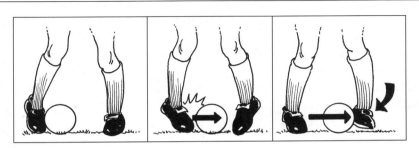

Soccer Boxing - One

In one spot - While dancing tap the ball from the inside of other foot.

Moving in Figure 8 - While dancing tap the ball from inside to inside and move left, right, backward and forward in figure 8.

Soccer Boxing - Two

In one spot - While dancing tap the ball from the inside of one foot to the instep of other foot. (Note: Turn instep towards ball).

Moving in Figure 8 - While dancing tap the ball from inside to instep and move left, right, backward and forward in figure 8.

More: The ball can also be tapped from one instep to the other while applying the above instructions.

Figure 8 Stretch Routine

Stretching: For the prevention of injuries, a coach must understand that a player's muscles are surrounded by a sheath of connective tissue called the epimysium. Unless the epimysium is allowed to expand, the muscles will be restricted from a full range of motion, and maximum work capacity from these hindered muscles cannot be expected. Forcing a player to jerk, jump, or run into a state of feeling loose can be harmful.

Objective: Allow muscles to stretch to their full range of motion. Create habit that may prevent injuries in the future.

Important: At appropriate moments during Figure 8, ask the players to do the following:

Ankle: Roll ball forward, hold toes up. Roll ball backward, hold toes down.

Calves: In a running start position, lock knee, shift body to lean forward and roll ball around leg and cone.

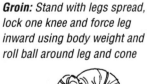

Groin: Stand with legs spread, lock one knee and force leg inward using body weight and roll ball around leg and cone

Figure 8 Stretch Routine

Stretching

Quads: Left leg behind the body, clasp hand around ankle. Roll ball around cone & leg with other hand.

Ham: Feet about shoulder-width apart and pointed straight ahead. Slowly bend forward. Roll ball around cone and legs.

Neck: Push head against hand-held-ball resistance (front, back, left and right side).

Stomach: In prone position, plant heels close to buttocks, bring upper body upward to touch forehead to ball.

Ruling principles:

- Alternate between Figure 8 and stretching.
- Hold at tension for brief moment and relax.
- All subsequent movements are beyond initial point.
- As players get older lengthen moments of stretch.
- Slow and easy. **No bouncing!**

Cooperative Phase   ⊞ = **P**layers **L**earn **U**sing **S**toppages

Players working in pairs to perfect an old Themes and learn a new Theme.

Objective: The main objective is to have players cooperate with each other and the coach in order to perfect a Theme.

Players:
- Work on old Themes to create instinctive responses to game situations.
- Learn a new Theme to resolve situations that may arise in the game.

Coach: Prepare to stop action and make 'points of refinement' on the Theme.

Coach: Make the players aware (teach them) that **stoppages** for coaching will take place during this phase of the practice.

Players **L**earn **U**sing **S**toppages

How the Field Must Look

It is the player's responsibility to lay out the field!

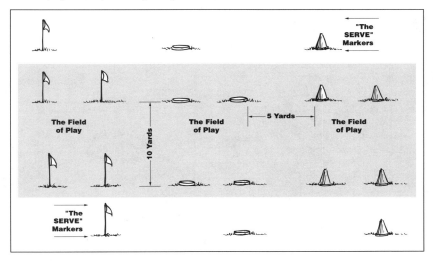

Remember:

- The distance between small goals and "The SERVE" markers depend on the skill level of your players.
- The players must be able to successfully PUSH and PEEK within the space between the goal and "The SERVE" markers, then PASS the ball.

How to Make a Small Goal

1. With feet together, hold objects in each outstretched hand.
2. Move right foot as far as you can. Place object outside right foot.
3. Bring feet back together.
4. Do the same thing on the left side.

5. There is your perfect small goal!

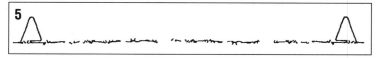

"The SERVE" Marker

How to Step Off Between Goals

10 yards or 10 giant steps.

How to Step Off Between Adjacent Goals

5 yards or 5 giant steps.

"The SERVE"

"The SERVE" was created specifically to provide the most efficient setting to learn attacking and defending techniques

Participants:
Receiver - the player without the ball, goes through the pattern with the intent of receiving the ball and becoming a Cooperative First Attacker.
Server - the player, with the ball, goes through the pattern with the intent of releasing the ball and becoming a Cooperative First Defender.

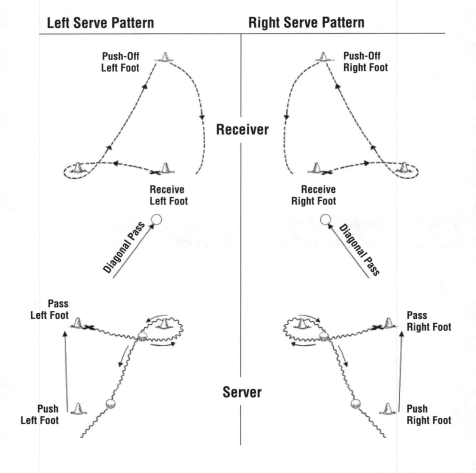

"The SERVE"

Patient, consistent-sequential exposure to "The SERVE" will realize and develop effective Attacking (see pages 96-102) and Defending (see pages 138-145) running off the ball habits in the Receiver.

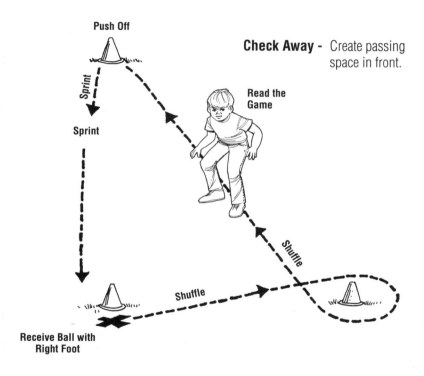

Check Away - Create passing space in front.

In the "Right Serve" pattern the Receiver will:

Read the Game - using their eyes to assess the situation.

Shuffle - moving in various directions while in the Ready Stance (see page 142).

Push-Off - change direction in anticipation of either intercepting or receiving the ball.

Sprint - change pace to adjust to the situation.

Receive the Ball - bring the ball under control with a classic first touch.

Become Cooperative First Attacker - after bringing the ball under control.

"The SERVE"

Patient, consistent-sequential exposure to "The SERVE" will realize and develop effective Dribbling (see pages 110-118) and Passing (see pages 130-133) habits in the Server.

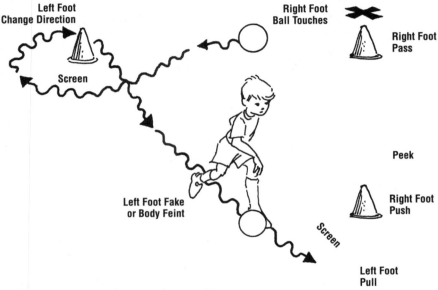

In the "Right Serve" pattern the Server will:

Ball Touches - use all parts of the right foot (see pages 111 & 112).

Screen - keep the body between the ball and cone (opponent).

Change Direction - use all parts of the left foot (see page 111 & 113).

Fake and Feints - fake with the feet and feint with the body (see pages 114 & 115).

Pull - turn with the ball using all parts of the left foot (see page 111 & 116.

Push - nudge the ball forward to create time to peek.

Peek - use your eyes to assess the situation.

Pass - release the ball diagonally to either space or feet.

Become Cooperative First Defender - after releasing the ball.

After "The SERVE"

After the **Receiver** runs the pattern:
- Meet the ball by getting into its path.
- Greet the ball with a slight hop on the plant foot.
- First touch ball with right foot if on right side of the goal.
- First touch ball with left foot if on left side of the goal.
  - Become cooperative first attacker during the ONE + ONE.
  - Become competitive first attacker during ONE vs. ONE.

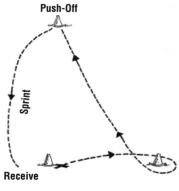

Server -

After the **Server** runs the pattern:
- Push, Peek and Diagonal Pass.
- Pass with right foot if on right side of the goal.
- Pass with left foot if on left side of the goal.
- Pass hard to feet.
- Pass soft to space.
  - Become cooperative first defender during the ONE + ONE.
  - Become competitive first defender during ONE vs. ONE.

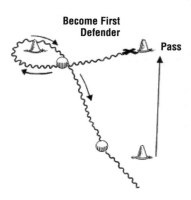

After "The SERVE"

How to cooperate after "The SERVE" using the Stages of Play.

Beginning Stage
- Perform 'Theme' at controlled speed vs. *walking opponent.*
- Environment that allows player to experiment with the 'Theme'.
- Allowing ample time to concentrate on perfect execution of the 'Theme'.
- At a speed where movement/action is slower to allow learning to take place.
- At distance from partner performing 'theme' where success is guaranteed.

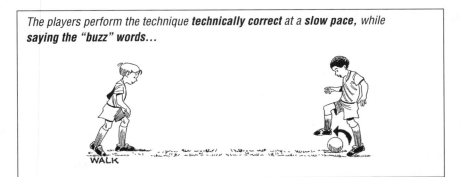

*The players perform the technique **technically correct** at a **slow pace**, while*
saying the "buzz" words...

WALK

Increasing the speed of movement and eliminating the "buzz" words is part of the progression as the players become more proficient.

After "The SERVE"

Intermediate Stage
- Perform 'Theme' at controlled speed vs. ***jogging opponent.***
- Environment that challenges player while experiment with the 'Theme'.
- Allowing player less time to concentrate on perfect execution of the 'Theme'.
- At speed where movement/action is faster to challenge learning taking place.
- At distance from partner performing 'theme' with probability of success.

Advanced Stage
- Perform 'Theme' at controlled speed vs. ***game speed opponent.***
- Environment that tests player while experimenting with the 'Theme'.
- Allowing player to concentrate on perfect execution of 'Theme' at game speed.
- At speed where movement/action is dictated by the pressure of the opponent.
- At distance from partner performing 'theme' where proper decision = success.

Coach:
- Some players may never get out of Beginning Stage - That is OK!
- Be careful when advancing player through Stages - Success is the Key!
- When in doubt put player back in previous Stage - Success is the Key!

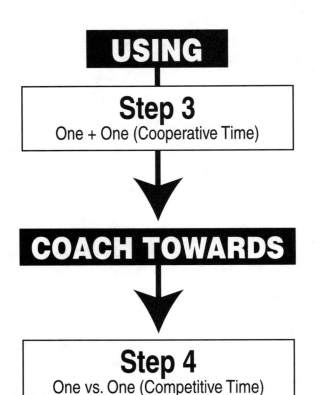

USING

Step 3
One + One (Cooperative Time)

COACH TOWARDS

Step 4
One vs. One (Competitive Time)

Teaching The ONE vs. ONE Game

Attack the opponent's goal as the first attacker. The duty of the first attacker is to score.

MEET by dribbling straight at the opponent.

GREET by foot fake or body feint.

BEAT by exploding past the opponent.

Defend one's own goal as the first defender. The duty of the first defender is to block the goal, then pressure the ball.

PEEK by finding your own goal.

MOVE to block the goal.

SEEK and pressure the ball.

Teaching The ONE vs. ONE Game

How to score points as the first attacker.

Some ideas:
- Score from only one side.
- Score from either side.
- Ball must roll between markers.
- Ball can bounce between markers.
- Ball must be dribbled through markers.
- Ball must be released from specific distance.
- Use your imagination!

How to score points as the first defender.

Some ideas:
- Score goal if attacker doesn't score in time limit.
- Score by taking ball away with 'poke' tackle.
- Score by taking ball away with 'block' tackle.
- Score by just taking the ball away.
- Use your imagination!

How the Game is Stopped - "The Signal"

1. Stop playing on 'signal'.
2. Get back to your goal as quickly as possible.
3. Last one back to own goal - gives opponent a point.

How to Report Individual Scores

- Keeps the elements of competition motivating play
- Allows players to catch their breath, for example:
  - Inactive rest period - all action stops as they stand next to goal.
  - Active rest period - light activity like passing ball back & forth.
- Keep tabs of individual progress.

How to Rotate

Getting ready to face the next opponent.

- Go to the next goal in a clockwise direction.
- Retrieve the ball to be served.
- Prepare to play the next opponent.

Competitive Phase   [VS] = Coach is **V**erbally **S**ilent

Players competing in pairs to perfect old Themes and test the new Theme.

Objective: To have players compete against each other while coach observes progress in Theme development.

Players:
- Perfect ability to perform old Themes vs. real opposition.
- Test ability to perform new Theme vs. real opposition.

Coach: Be verbally silent and observe individuals ability to perform old and new Themes vs. real opposition.

Competitive play.

In ONE vs. ONE game, play must be continuous. To assure this, the fields must have no boundaries.

Coach: Make the players aware (teach them) that **no stoppages** for coaching will take place during this phase of the practice.

Coach be **V**erbally **S**ilent

Playing the ONE vs. ONE Game

LET THEM PLAY — The ONE vs. ONE GAME

- Begin the game with **"The SERVE" from the right side.**

- Duration of each game depends on age group and fitness:
  - Young = 15 - 30 seconds
  - Older = 30 - 60 seconds
  - It is not recommended to exceed 60 seconds

- Race back to starting point when time is over.

- Report score to coach/score keeper.

- Don't forget the inactive and active rest period.

- Rotate and prepare to play the next opponent.

- Continue this sequence until every player has played everyone on the team. Begin **'new'** sequence with **"The SERVE" from the left side.**

Accumulation of points may be used to motivate players to work harder:

- To become Co-Captains.

- To be in the starting line-up.

- To show improvement.

Practice Your Half-Time Routine

- Gather the team in a defined, secluded, shaded area.

- Encourage and have players replenish liquids.

- Check for injuries.

- Teach players 'how to' relax and communicate with each other.

- Seek feedback from individual players.

- Give points of refinement (if necessary) to:
  - Individuals (privately)
  - Group
  - Team

- Review the 'Theme'
  - Give another demonstration/explanation of 'theme' (if necessary)
  - Give a demonstration explanation of using 'theme' vs. more opposition

- Prepare them for the 2nd half of practice.

- Show enthusiasm and support!

Playing Small Sided Games

These games are framed within a set of rules to correct or improve on the "Theme".

- Involve maximum number of players in a minimum amount of space.

- Allow maximum touches of the ball in minimum amount of time.

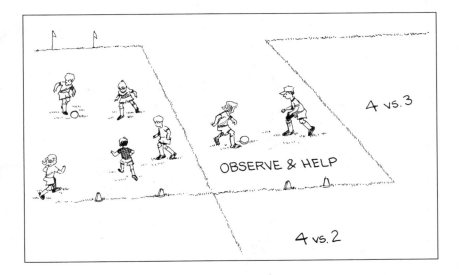

Small Sided Games create an atmosphere where technique can be observed under game related conditions.

- Allow the coach opportunities to coach without disrupting others.

- Create competitive atmosphere resulting in improving physical fitness, technique and variety to keep players interested.

There are two types of Small Sided Games: Cooperative and Competitive.

Cooperative Small Sided Games

- Controlled by the coach.
- Players understand that the Coach *may stop* or interrupt play to make "Points of Refinement".

Players **L**earn **U**sing **S**toppages

Competitive Small Sided Games

- **'Free'** games controlled by the players.
- Players understand that the Coach ***will not stop*** or interrupt play to make "Points of Refinement".
- Coach is Verbally Silent.

Helpful Hints:
- – Discipline yourself to know when to leave the players alone!
- – Over coaching can often be worse than no coaching!
- – Be careful, that in the haste of competing, technique does not deteriorate.
- – Recognize fatigue and when it becomes a factor in learning.
- – Include active/inactive rest periods when the activity is at a high pace.

When in doubt **go back to basics.** When things are not working, slow down the action.

Coach be

There are two catagories of Small Sided Games: Even and Uneven.

Even Small Sided Games

- Teams of equal number...such as 1v1; 2v2; 3v3; 4v4; 5v5; etc.
- Are used primarily to improve all techniques *except passing.*

Uneven Small Sided Games

- Teams of unequal numbers, such as 5v0; 4v1; 3v2; 2v1; 7v4; etc.
- Are used primarily to *improve passing.*

Example: 4 vs. 0 = Beginning Passers
4 vs. 1 = Weak Passers
4 vs. 2 = Average Passers
4 vs. 3 = Sure Passers

Specific Rules for team with larger numbers.

- Each member is restricted to 'two-touch' play.
  - 1st Touch = Control
  - 2nd Touch = Pass
- Infraction of 'two-touch' rule
  - Lose possession of the ball or
  - Opponent is given a goal.
- Scoring: Putting ball through goal or
  - Reaching specific number of consecutive passes without opponent interceptions. (Ex: 5 consecutive passes = goal)

Specific Rules for team with smaller numbers.

- Each member of the team is allowed to dribble.
  - Discourage first time kicks.
- Scoring: Putting ball through the goal or
  - Intercepting and controlling passes by the larger team.

Important:
Increase the size of smaller team as skill level in passing advances.

Size of Playing Area

- **Technically Weak** – More space to guarantee success!

- **Technically Stronger** – Smaller playing area to increase pressure.

- **Attacking Theme** – Wider field, more space for attacking success.

- **Defending Theme** – Narrower field, less space for defending success.

Remember to apply the "Formula for the Length".
(1) vs. 1 = 1 player x 10 = 10 yards long
(3) vs. 2 = 3 player x 10 = 30 yards long
(5) vs. 3 = 5 player x 10 = 50 yards long

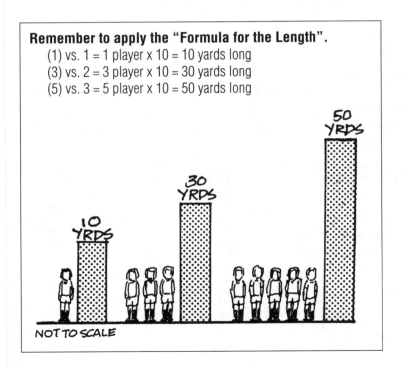

NOT TO SCALE

Number of Opponents

- **Technically Weaker** – Fewer opponents to guarantee success!

- **Technically Stronger** – More opponents to create a challenge!

Number of Balls

Two or more balls in play.

- Creates more touches with the ball.
- Forces players to work on the **Peeking** technique.
- More opportunities to score goals.
- Adds variety and fun!

Number of Goals

Using Two Goals

Two small goals.

Parallel goals.

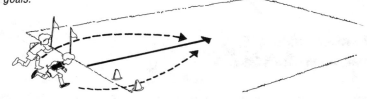

Players as goals.

Objective: Attack by passing ball between opponents' spread legs.

Note: Rotate players by calling switch' every minute.

One Regulation Goal - One small goal.

Two Regulation Goals.

Number of Goals

Using Three Goals

Mid-field goals: Score from any direction.

Three small goals.

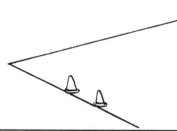
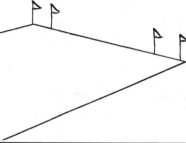

One regulation - two small goals.

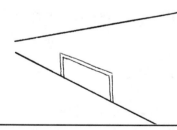
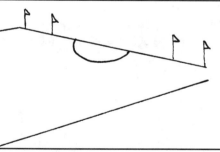

Three regulation goals.

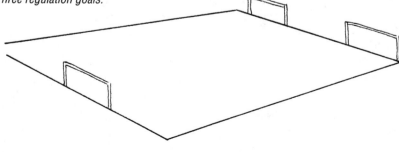

Number of Goals

Using Four Goals

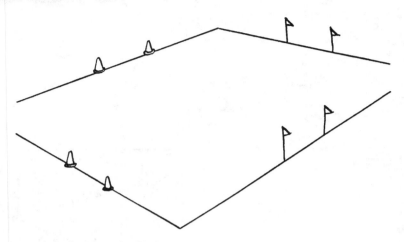

Example: One team Attacks the flag goals and Defends cones.
Opponent Attacks the cone goals and Defends flags.

Five or more goals.
Objective: A goal is scored when ball goes through goal and is controlled by a teammate.

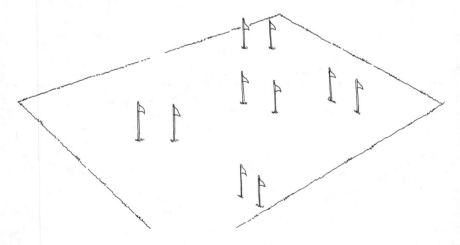

Rules You Can Use

Silent Soccer – No one is allowed to talk, yell, etc., during the game!

Specify One Foot at a Time, Right or Left Foot Only – Foot limitation games are aimed at developing players' weak foot.

Specify Part of Shoe – That must be used to receive, dribble or release ball. Example: Instep Only!

Height Limitation – Below knee, chin, head. Example: Ball may not leave the ground.

Everyone Will Play – Specify # of players that must touch the ball before the team can attempt to score. Example: (6v4) Five of the six must touch before scoring attempts.

Neutral Player – Sides with team in control of the ball (theme: attack). Sides with team not in control of ball (theme: defense)

Be Creative – Examples:
- Goal for beating opponent with specific fake or feint.
- Goal for successful combination play, example: "Give and Go".
- Goal for good 'poke' tackle.
- Goal for forcing ball over touch line.
- Goal for good sportsmanship.
- Goal for helping with the equipment.
- Goal for (use your imagination)!

Important: Make up rules that create an atmosphere where the player(s) must work on the 'theme' or their particular weakness.

Very Important: To be effective any infraction of the rules must result in immediate, loss of ball possession, goal for the opponent or both loss of ball and goal for opponent.

Number of Ball Touches

• **One Touch** = Shooting in Attack
  - Attacking Team is limited to ONE-touch play (hopefully toward goal), once ball goes inside the area marked out by the coach.
  - Cones mark 'shooting range' boundary

Note: If few goals are being scored, then mark 'Shooting Range' closer to goal. If scoring becomes too easy, then mark 'Shooting Range' farther from goal.

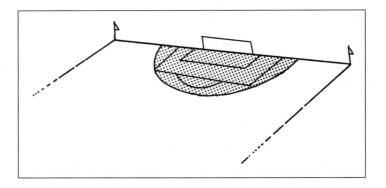

• **One Touch** = Clearing in Defense
  - Defending Team is limited to ONE-touch play (hopefully away from goal), once ball goes inside marked out area.
  - Cones mark 'Clearing Range' boundary.

Note: If players are technically weak, allow them to just kick the ball away. If players are technically strong, give them a target player or area to hit.

Number of Ball Touches

• Two Touch Play
Ball Control and Passing
- Ideally, 1st touch brings the ball under
  control.
- And 2nd touch results in a pass to a
  teammate.

• Three or More Touches
Dribbling, Foot Faking, Body Feinting, Screening, etc.

Note: Technically weak players are given fewer touches before being allowed to pass or shoot.
Technically strong players are given more touches before being allowed to pass or shoot.
Increase number of touches with ball according to each player's skill level.

Very Important:
  • Infraction of one, two, three or more touch rule results in:
    - Loss of ball possession or...
    - Goal for the opponent or...
    - Both, loss of ball and goal for opponent.

Sample Games

Goalie Rotation

Number of Players:	2 vs. 2 and 2 vs. 2
Field of Play:	40 yards long.
Objective:	Attack and Defend as a Team.
Rules:	Two players begin on goal line – two partners in field. Play two minutes – Keepers and field players change at 'switch' call.

Restriction: Keepers must stay on goal line and may not use their hands.

Note: Keep accurate time for 'switch' call.

Sample Games

All Must Hustle

Number of players: Two equal teams.

Objective: Team can score **only** when all players of that team are across the half-way line.

Note: Stay on half-way line to observe infractions

No Goal!

Goal!

Important: Be creative, utilize rules that create an atmosphere where the player may work on his particular weakness.

There are two types of scrimmages: Cooperative and Competitive.

Cooperative Scrimmage
Controlled by the Coach.

- A *full team* game framed inside a set of rules to focus on the theme.

- Players understand that the Coach *may stop or interrupt play* to make "Points of Refinement".

Use ideas introduced in the Small Sided Games section when playing the cooperative scrimmage.

*P*layers *L*earn *U*sing *S*toppages

Important: Be creative - utilize rules that create an atmosphere where each player must work on his particular weakness.

Competitive Scrimmage

Controlled by the Players.

The Competitive Scrimmage is a "free" game that allows the team to solve any problems with the Coach **Verbally Silent.**

Players:
- Players understand that the Coach **will not stop or interrupt play** to make "Points of Refinement".

Coach:
- Discipline yourself to know when to leave the players alone!

Coach: Observe and take mental or written notes. Practice your game behavior on the sideline and never enter the field of play.

Important: Over coaching can often be worse than no coaching!

More Ways to Coach

1. **Ghost Soccer**
   a. Team **vs. no one** (shadow training) – coach specifies pass & running routes.
   b. Team **vs. time** (against stopwatch).

2. **Thinking - Out Loud Soccer**
   Coach calls out passes, shots, running routes etc.
   Create running patterns.

   Good - If infrequent calls by someone who knows the game (not idle chatter).
   Bad- If used too often, players will not learn to think for themselves.

3. Freeze Game

On a pre-arranged signal everyone stops.

To ..*rectify faults immediately, instant feedback.*
..avoid possible mistake coming up.
..avoid the situation to change drastically.
..allow the players to recall the situation.

4. Dead Ball Situation - Coaching

Coach recreates the situation when the ball is not in play. Make sure you observed what you will talk about. Be specific, do not ramble. Tailor your talk to the age group you are working with, be simple.

Helpful Hints:

Do not be sidetracked by other mistakes and stick to your Theme.
Do not abuse these games, create a flow in the action.

> **Very Important:**
> In all cases restart the action with the correct move or maneuver.

Physical Cool-Down

Many coaches fail to remember the tremendous physical/mental punishment their players must endure during practice and game situations. The cool-down period must become an integral part of every coach's training/playing routine.

The **physical** goal is to relieve the tightness created by running and other soccer related activities. Stress on the lower back is compounded by the unnatural kicking movements and jarring effects from landing on the solid surface of the playing field resulting in a narrowing of the spinal vertebrae. Stretching the spine and opening the narrowed spaces are necessary. A slow jog and some stretching exercises are sufficient for this training phase.

FUNdamental Cool-Down Routine:

1) ANKLE:
Outline alphabet with the toes.

2) GROIN:
Stand with legs spread, lock one knee, and force leg inward using body weight.

3) CALVES:
In running start position, lock knee, shift body to lean forward.

4) QUADS:
Left leg behind the body, clasp hand around ankle.

Physical Cool-Down

5) HAM:
Feet about shoulder-width apart and pointed straight ahead. Slowly bend forward.

6) BACK:
Indian style sitting touch forehead to the toes.

7) STOMACH:
In prone position, plant heels close to buttocks, bring upper body upward until the back is flat on the ground. Hold at least to 8 count.

8) NECK:
Push head against hand resistance.
(front, back, left and right side)

Important: To prevent soreness and injury...stretches should be done after every practice and game. If you are going to stretch only once, afterwards, is the most important time.

Mental Cool-Down

The **mental** goal is to relieve the tension created by spectators, peers or personal mistakes. After a practice the player must feel prepared for the next game. After a poor practice a feeling of accomplishment, not failure, must be created. After a good practice, players must be made aware that more improvement can take place.

- Summarize practice session and theme
- Briefly analyze the strong and weak points of their performance
- End with a positive statement which lets them know they improved.

> **Important:**
> 1. No public humiliation, ever!
> 2. Encouragement helps to increase natural enthusiasm.
> 3. Coaches must encourage effort, not results.

THE FLOW

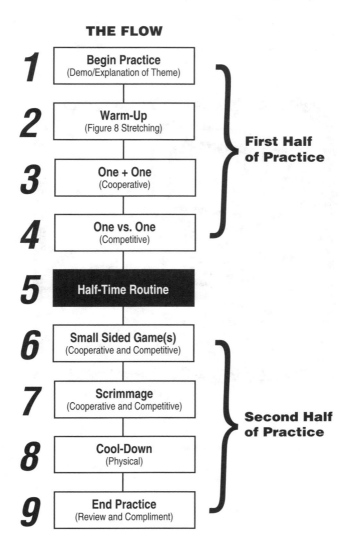

1 Begin Practice
(Demo/Explanation of Theme)

2 Warm-Up
(Figure 8 Stretching)

3 One + One
(Cooperative)

4 One vs. One
(Competitive)

**First Half
of Practice**

5 Half-Time Routine

6 Small Sided Game(s)
(Cooperative and Competitive)

7 Scrimmage
(Cooperative and Competitive)

8 Cool-Down
(Physical)

9 End Practice
(Review and Compliment)

**Second Half
of Practice**

Guarantee:
Patient, consistent-sequential exposure to this FUNdamental practice routine will produce real results.

Visit our website:
FUNdamentalsoccer.com
for exchanging great ideas!

FUNdamental Soccer

Section 4

Attacking Themes

Peeking

OBJECTIVE: To realize and develop the habit of effective **'Peeking'** while attacking.

STEP 1 - Begin Practice with Explanation and Demonstration
- At first practice introduce the 'buzz words' Push - **Peek** - Push.
- Push - the ball a proper distance forward. Eyes on the ball.
- **Peek** - Eyes up to read the game.
- Push - the ball a proper distance forward. Eyes on the ball.
- At second practice introduce the phrase "Ball in flight - **Peek** left and right."

That is, anytime the ball is travelling between players, **Peek** - to see:
- Where am I on the field?
- Where is the goal to attack?
- Where are my teammates?
- Where are the opponents?
- Can I shoot when I receive the ball?

STEP 2 - Warm-Up
- Practice **Peeking** during the Figure 8 Stretch Routine.
- Teach them:

Eyes up to see it all.

Eyes down to touch the ball.

Peeking

STEP 3 - ONE + ONE (Cooperative Time)
   - "The SERVE" compels practice of the **Peeking** technique.

Push Off

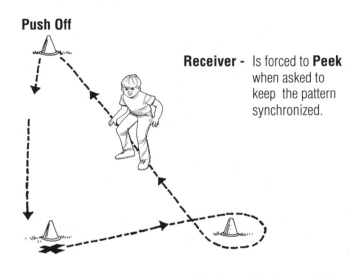

Receiver - Is forced to **Peek** when asked to keep the pattern synchronized.

Server - Asked to push the ball and **Peek** throughout the serving pattern.

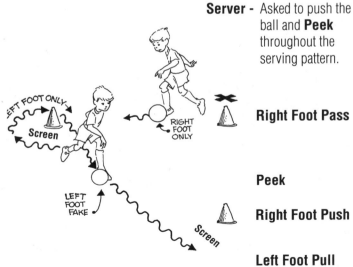

Right Foot Pass

Peek

Right Foot Push

Left Foot Pull

Peeking　　STEP 3 *Continued*

Push Off

Receiver - Peek for opponent's actions, then locate the travelling ball.

"Ball in flight, **Peek** left and right."

Server - Peek to find your goal, then seek the ball as it travels.

LEFT FOOT ONLY

Screen

RIGHT FOOT ONLY

Right Foot Pass

Peek

LEFT FOOT FAKE

Screen

Right Foot Push

Left Foot Pull

Instruction:

Both players are to **Peek** left and right and take their eyes off the ball while the ball is travelling between the players.

Peeking

STEP 4 - ONE vs. ONE
- Begin all games with "The SERVE".
- "The SERVE" provides an ideal setting for disguising the repetitious practice of the **Peeking** technique.

STEP 5 - Half-Time Routine
- Water and relax.
- Review Explanation/Demonstration of **Peeking**.

STEP 6 - Small Sided Games (Cooperative and Competitive)
- Teach and encourage **Peeking**.

STEP 7 - Scrimmage (Cooperative and Competitive)
- Teach and encourage **Peeking**.

STEP 8 - Cool-Down
- Review **Peeking** technique

STEP 9 - End of Practice
- Compliment each player's improvement in **Peeking!**

Moving

OBJECTIVE: To realize and develop the habit of effective **'Moving'** while attacking.

STEP 1 - Begin Practice with Explanation and Demonstration
- Teach them 'how to' **move** to help teammates by:
- Getting into a position to receive the ball.
- Getting rid of the opponent in order to receive a pass.
- Making it difficult for the opponent to see both the ball and them at the same time.

STEP 2 - Warm-Up
- Practice deceptive **Moving** in the Figure 8 Stretch Routine.
- Moving forwards, backwards, shuffling, foot faking and body feinting!

STEP 3 - ONE + ONE (Cooperative Time)
- Adjust "The SERVE" to practice proper running patterns. For example, **check away** and create passing space in front.

Moving

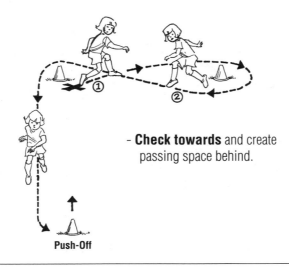

- **Check towards** and create passing space behind.

Push-Off

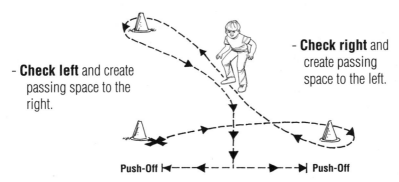

- **Check left** and create passing space to the right.

- **Check right** and create passing space to the left.

Push-Off |◄── ◄ ─┆─ ► ──►| Push-Off

Receiver - in appropriate stage of play:
Beginning - walking through pattern.
Intermediate - jogging through pattern.
Advanced - at speed through pattern.

Server - **Peek** to see type of Check Run receiver is running.
Pass 'soft to space' or 'hard to feet' and become cooperative first defender.

Moving

STEP 4 - ONE vs. ONE
- Begin every game with 'The Serve' .
- "The SERVE" is adjusted and disguises the repetitious practice of these **movements.**

STEP 5 - Half-Time Routine
- Water and relax.
- Review Explanation/Demonstration of **Moving**.

STEP 6 - Small Sided Games (Cooperative and Competitive)
- Teach and encourage **Moving.**

STEP 7 - Scrimmage (Cooperative and Competitive)
- Teach and encourage **Moving.**

STEP 8 - Cool-Down
- Review **Moving** technique

STEP 9 - End of Practice
- Compliment each player's improvement in **Moving!**

First Touch - Rolling Ball

OBJECTIVE: To realize and develop the habit of effective **'First Touch Play'**.

STEP 1 - Begin Practice with Explanation and Demonstration

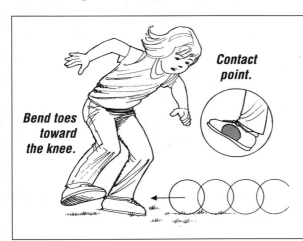

Contact point.

Bend toes toward the knee.

- Meet the ball by getting in its path.
- Bring the **inside of shoe** into the path of the ball.
- Lift receiving foot slightly off the ground.
- Hop on plant foot prior to moment of impact with the ball.
- Use relaxed 'Monkey Stance' - knees unlocked.

- Meet the ball by getting in its path.
- Bring the **outside of shoe** into the path of the ball.
- Lift receiving foot slightly off the ground.
- Hop on plant foot prior to moment of impact with the ball.
- Use relaxed 'Monkey Stance' - knees unlocked.

Contact point.

Point one big toe toward the other big toe.

First Touch - Rolling Ball

STEP 3 - One + One
Cooperative Time

Push Off

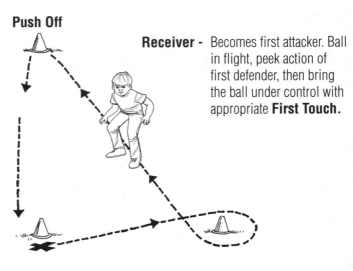

Receiver - Becomes first attacker. Ball in flight, peek action of first defender, then bring the ball under control with appropriate **First Touch.**

First Touch

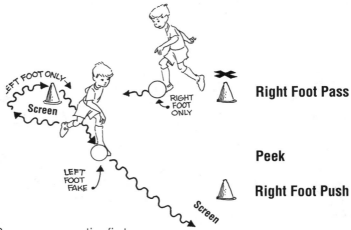

Right Foot Pass

Peek

Right Foot Push

Left Foot Pull

Server - Becomes cooperative first defender. Approach by walking, jogging or at speed to assure success and challenge. For first attacker practicing **First Touch.**

First Touch - Rolling Ball

STEP 2 - Warm-Up
- Practice touching the ball with **inside** and **outside of shoe** during the Figure 8 Stretch Routine.

STEP 3 - ONE + ONE (Cooperative Time) *see opposite page*
- Adapt 'The Serve' to fixate on the practice of **'First Touch Play'.**

STEP 4 - ONE vs. ONE
- Begin every game with 'The Serve' .
- "The SERVE" provides an ideal setting for disguised repetitious practice of **First Touch.**

STEP 5 - Half-Time Routine
- Water and relax.
- Review Explanation/Demonstration of **First Touch Play.**

STEP 6 - Small Sided Games (Cooperative and Competitive)
- **Use Two-Touch Rule** to encourage proper First Touch.

STEP 7 - Scrimmage (Cooperative and Competitive)
- **Use Two-Touch Rule** to encourage proper First Touch.

STEP 8 - Cool-Down
- Review **First Touch** technique.

STEP 9 - End of Practice
- Compliment each player's improvement in **First Touch Play!**

First Touch - Ball in Flight

OBJECTIVE: To realize and develop the habit of effective **'First Touch Play'**.

STEP 1 - Begin Practice with Explanation and Demonstration
- Teach them 'how to' move quickly to bring controlling surface into the flight of the ball.
- Stay on those toes and keep those feet moving.
- Receiving foot is slightly off the ground, like a metal detector.
- Place 'toe-section' over anticipated spot where the ball will bounce.
- Hop on plant foot just prior to movement of impact with the ball.

Slightly off the ground like a "metal detector".

Contact point.

"Like a metal detector searching for an ounce, toes over the spot where the ball will bounce."

- Teach your players, *"If possible, let no ball bounce"*.

First Touch - Ball in Flight

STEP 2 - Warm-Up
   - Practice bringing flighted ball under control during Figure 8 Stretch Routine.

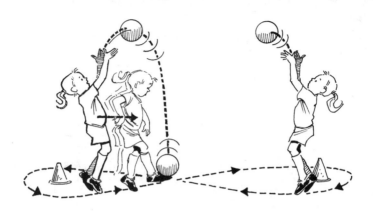

STEP 3 - ONE + ONE (Cooperative Time)
   - Adapt "The SERVE" to focus on the practice of **'First Touch Play'**.

Receiver - Becomes first attacker. Ball in flight, peek action of first defender, then bring ball under control with appropriate **First Touch.**

First Touch - Ball in Flight

STEP 3 - ONE + ONE (Cooperative Time)
  - The server becomes cooperative first defender. Dribble through pattern using
    Push, Pick-up and Throw-in sequence.
  - Approach by walking, jogging or at speed to assure success and challenge for
    first attacker practicing **First Touch Play**.

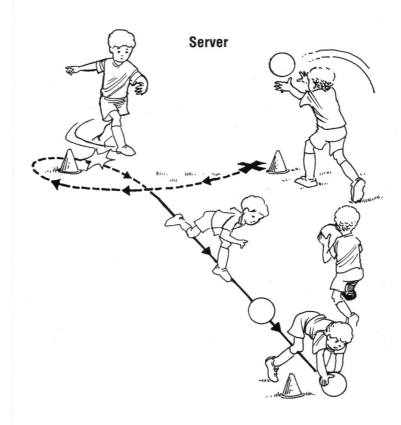

Server

First Touch - Ball in Flight

STEP 4 - ONE vs. ONE
- Begin every game with "The SERVE".
- "The SERVE" provides an ideal setting for disguised repetitious practice of the **First Touch** theme.

STEP 5 - Half-Time Routine
- Water and relax.
- Review Explanation/Demonstration of **First Touch Play**.

STEP 6 - Small Sided Games (Cooperative and Competitive)
- **Restart all action with a high toss or throw-in** to encourage First Touch Play.

STEP 7 - Scrimmage (Cooperative and Competitive)
- **Restart all action with a high toss or throw-in** to encourage First Touch Play.

STEP 8 - Cool-Down
- Review **First Touch** technique

STEP 9 - End of Practice
- Compliment each player's improvement in **First Touch Play!**

CAUTION: When teaching control of a flighted ball, fear of pain must be taken into consideration. The young player often sees a harmful projectile flying at him, not the soccer ball. Confidence building must be the first procedure in teaching control of flighted balls. The height of the toss can eliminate some of the fears, low at first, then increase the height to develop technique.

Dribbling

OBJECTIVE: To realize and develop the habit of effective **'Dribbling'**.

STEP 1 - Begin Practice with Explanation and Demonstration

Keeping the ball under control, as defined in this book, is the art of maneuvering the ball with the feet in order to maintain ball possession **against an opponent.** Much of the skill amounts to the ability to control the ball while running, stopping and turning at various speeds. Deceptive body movements in combination with foot maneuvers are used to beat the opponent.

- An effective ball handler can:
  - Keep the ball until a teammate is in a clear position to receive a pass.
  - Get past a defender thus gaining numerical superiority on the attack.
  - Clear oneself for a shot on goal.

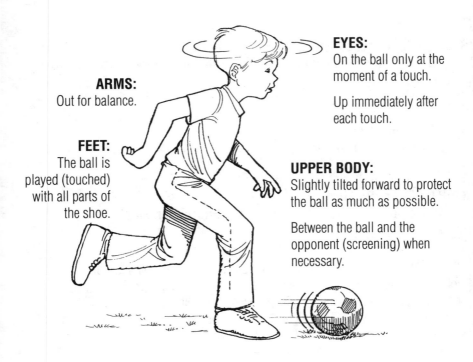

EYES:
On the ball only at the moment of a touch.

Up immediately after each touch.

ARMS:
Out for balance.

FEET:
The ball is played (touched) with all parts of the shoe.

UPPER BODY:
Slightly tilted forward to protect the ball as much as possible.

Between the ball and the opponent (screening) when necessary.

STEP 1 - Explanation and Demonstration

IN when space is thin.

(Inside of shoe)

OUT to get about.

(Outside of shoe)

IN and **OUT** in a crowd.

Use the **LACES**...

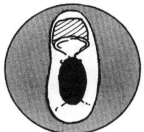

...to drive through spaces.

It's for real you can use the **HEEL**.

Use the **SOLE** to make it whole.

If it works - it is right!

Zig-Zag Patterns

- Encourage touches with the ball on every stride:
- Rhythm of Tap-step-Tap-step-Tap....

Zig-Zag Pattern Left Foot Two-Touch Play:
Sequence: Touch twice outside left.
Touch twice inside left.
Continue by repeating.

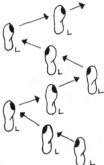

Zig-Zag Pattern Right Foot Two-Touch Play:
Sequence: Touch twice outside right.
Touch twice inside right.
Continue by repeating.

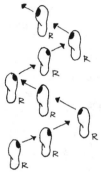

Zig-Zag Pattern Alternating Feet One-Touch Play: (Start Left)
Sequence: Touch once outside left.
Touch once inside left. Touch once
outside right. Touch once inside right.
Continue by repeating.

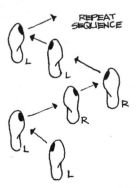

Zig-Zag Pattern Alternating Feet One-Touch Play: (Start Right)
Sequence: Touch once outside right.
Touch once inside right. Touch once
outside left. Touch once inside left.
Continue by repeating.

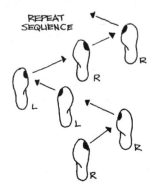

Changing Directions

Push, Stop, Step and Change Directions.

Push *Stop* *Step* *Change Direction*

Push, Tap and Change Direction:

Tap the ball across the body.

Push *Tap* *Change Direction*

Attacking Fakes

All attacking fakes should include the following three requirements:
  a. Approach opponent at moderate speed.
  b. Give opponent impression that the ball is moving favorably in his direction.
  c. Quickly accelerate past the opponent .

Right Foot Fake...Left Foot Take Series

Right Foot Besides:

First Movement - Step right foot fake toward the opponent even with the ball. Dipping left shoulder for extra effect...

Second Movement - With outside of left foot (take) ball past the opponent.

Left Foot Over:

First Movement - Pretend to pass the ball with outside of left foot. Bringing left foot (fake) over the ball...and toward the opponent.

Second Movement - With outside of right foot (take) ball past the opponent.

Important: Practice these movements in both left and right directions.

Deceptive Moves

Important: While practicing these moves keep in mind that the body is to stay between the opponent and the ball (shielding).

Stop and Explode:
First Movement - Straight line dribble - moderate speed. Slap sole on ball and stop.
Second Movement - Read the field Determine where free space exists. Explode into that direction.

Locomotive:
First Movement - Fake placing sole on the ball.
And "explode" past frozen opponent.

Turns

Hook-Turn:

First Movement - Straight line dribble - moderate speed. Hook instep around the ball.
Second Movement - Swivel on bottom of left foot. Move in opposite direction.

Fake-Hook-Turn:

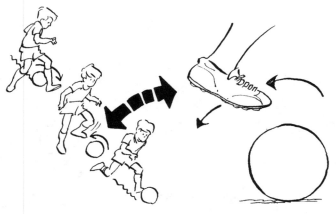

First Movement – Same as above except, **do not touch the ball.**

Second Movement – Pull foot immediately back from the ball. "Explode" past the opponent.

Extremely Important: Introduce only one of these movements at a time! Players must practice all these movements in both left and right directions.

Dribbling

STEP 2 - Warm-Up
- Figure 8 Stretch Routine is ideal for practicing **keeping ball under control**.

STEP 3 - ONE + ONE (Cooperative Time)
- Use "The SERVE" to further ingrain **keeping ball under control**.

Receiver - Becomes first attacker. Run through pattern and bring ball under control. Practice **keeping ball under control** vs. cooperative first defender.

Server - Becomes cooperative first defender. Challenge first attacker but allow success by applying stages of play. Walk, jog or at speed.

---

*The players perform the technique **technically correct** at a **slow pace**, while **saying the "buzz" words**...*

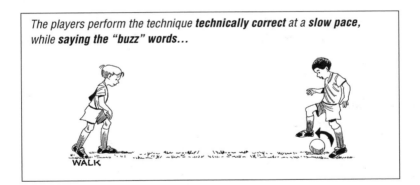

WALK

Dribbling

STEP 4 - ONE vs. ONE
- Begin every game with "The SERVE".
- "The SERVE" further ingrains **keeping ball under control** confidence.

STEP 5 - Half-Time Routine
- Water and relax.
- Review Explanation/Demonstration of **keeping ball under control.**

STEP 6 - Small Sided Games (Cooperative and Competitive)
- Apply the **Three or More Touch Rule** to enforce keeping ball under control.

STEP 7 - Scrimmage (Cooperative and Competitive)
- Apply the **Three or More Touch Rule** to enforce keeping ball under control.

STEP 8 - Cool-Down
- Review **keeping ball under control** technique.

STEP 9 - End of Practice
- Compliment each player's improvement in **keeping ball under control!**

Shooting

OBJECTIVE: To realize and develop the habit of effective **'shooting'**.

STEP 1 - Begin Practice with Explanation and Demonstration

Scoring goals is what the game of soccer is all about. It is actually FUN to be able to score a goal, if in practice or in the game. The most widely used technique used for this purpose is the instep kick, which consists of:

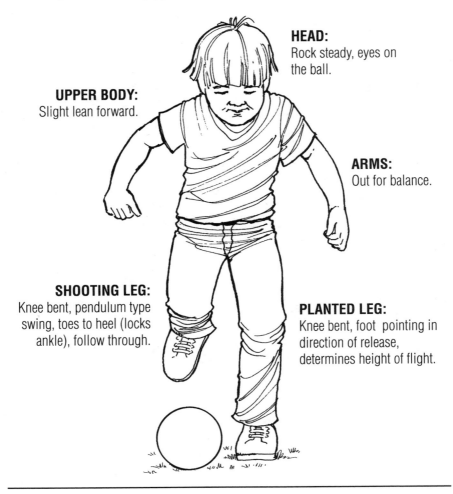

HEAD:
Rock steady, eyes on the ball.

UPPER BODY:
Slight lean forward.

ARMS:
Out for balance.

SHOOTING LEG:
Knee bent, pendulum type swing, toes to heel (locks ankle), follow through.

PLANTED LEG:
Knee bent, foot pointing in direction of release, determines height of flight.

Shooting

STEP 1 - Explanation and Demonstration

Contact Point

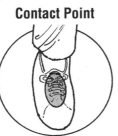

Toes Down

Bent Toes
towards the heel
which locks the ankle.

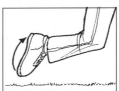

Planted Foot
even with ball results
in low ball flight.

Hop - Step

Planted Foot
behind the ball results
in high ball flight.

Hop - Step

The approach: Slightly from the side (angular).

Shooting

STEP 2 - Warm-Up
- Use **Push-Peek-Push** sequence during Figure 8 Stretch Routine.
- **Push** ball (instep only) proper distance forward. Eyes on the ball.
- **Peek** Eyes up to see it all!
- **Push** ball (instep only) proper distance forward. Eyes on the ball.

Push Off

STEP 3 - ONE + ONE
(Cooperative Time)
- Adjust "The SERVE" to practice instep only ball touches.

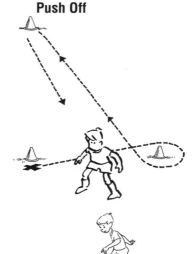

Receiver - Becomes goalkeeper. Run through pattern and become cooperative goalkeeper.

Server - Practices shooting technique. Take ball through pattern with instep touches only. Push ball a proper distance forward. Eyes on the ball. Peek to find the open net. Place (instep kick) the ball into the open net.

LEFT FOOT ONLY

Screen

RIGHT FOOT ONLY

Pass

LEFT FOOT FAKE

Screen

Peek

Push

Pull

Shooting

STEP 4 - ONE vs. ONE
- Begin every game with "The SERVE".
- "The SERVE" is adjusted and disguises the repetitious practice of the **shooting technique.**
- Include a ONE vs. Goalkeeper game into this step.

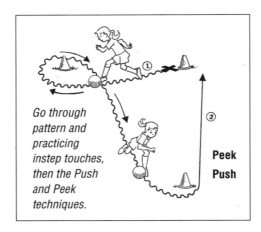

Go through pattern and practicing instep touches, then the Push and Peek techniques.

Peek

Push

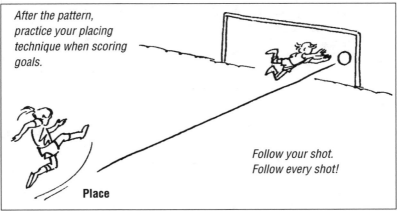

After the pattern, practice your placing technique when scoring goals.

Follow your shot. Follow every shot!

Place

Keep track of the number of goals scored within a given time limit.

Realistic Shooting

Do not use stationary balls as part of shooting practice.

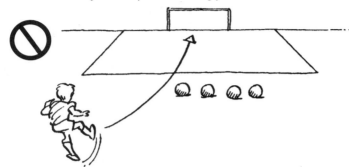

Unless *players are shooting around a wall,*

or *taking penalty shots.*

Important:
Shooting practices become beneficial when they resemble game conditions.

Theme: Release the Ball

Self Serve

Against a wall.

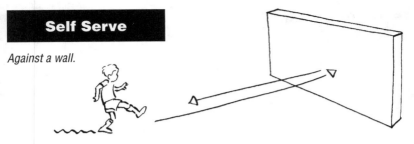

*Regulation goal size with **no goalkeeper.***

Do an exercise. Example: Forward Roll or Push-up before taking immediate shot.

Dribble away from goal through slalom. Turn 180 using hook turn. Take immediate shoot.

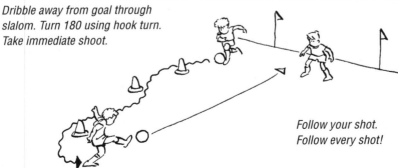

Follow your shot. Follow every shot!

Reminder: Have them 'follow' each and every shot!

Self Serve

Go around an obstacle.
Take immediate shot.

Jump over obstacle. Take immediate shot.

Direction Shooting: *Coach points which side shot is to be taken.*

Don't Forget: Have them 'follow' each and every shot!

Partner Serve

Only after the player has mastered the art of instep kick (self serve) should the coach introduce a working partner (partner serve). The level of difficulty to execute each instep shot increases depending on the point of origin of the pass.

Three types of serves may be given:

1. Through Pass – *the least difficult.*

Note: *Take a large stride ahead of the ball with plant foot. This allows the ball to roll into a low kick position.*

2. Backward Pass

Note: *Make contact through the middle or slightly above the mid-line of the ball...very little follow through.*

3. Across Pass – *the most difficult.*

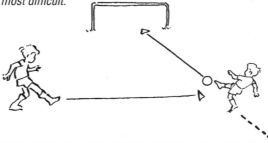

Common requirements to perfect these three kicks:
- Concentrate on accuracy.
- Keep the head down and steady.
- Strike through the middle or top half of the ball.

Partner Serve

Around the Server:
Step 1 - The kicker sprints around each server.
Step 2 -"Shooter" runs around server who passes ball into penalty area.
Step 3 -"Shooter" takes One-Touch shot on goal.
Step 4 -Continue sequence by going around next server.

Variations: Increase distance or servers from goal. Timed event with points for goals scored. Contest among players.

Pressure Shooting:
Step 1 - Shooter stands inside Penalty area and One-Touches ball being served.
Step 2 - Next server passes ball at the moment previous ball crosses goal line.

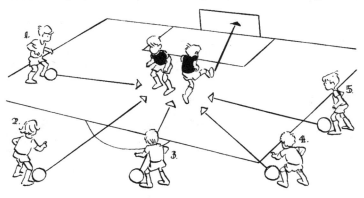

Variation: Serve ball in sequence. Serve ball at random.

Partner Serve

Number Shooting: (One vs. One)
Step 1 - Split team into two equal groups.
Step 2 - Give correspondent number to each pair of players.
Step 3 - Coach calls a number and passes the ball into play.
Step 4 - Players whose number is called challenge for the ball, and a shot on goal.
Note: Keep score.

Number(s) Shooting: (Small Sided Games)
Step 1 and 2 - Same as above.
Step 3 - Coach calls two or more numbers.
Step 4 - Those 'called' challenge the same numbers from opposing side.
Note: Keep score.

Variation:
Move groups farther away from the ball.
Players must do exercise before challenging for ball, like a push-up.

STEP 5 - Half-Time Routine
- Water and relax.
- Review Explanation/Demonstration of the **shooting technique.**

STEP 6 - Small Sided Games (Cooperative and Competitive)
- Apply the **One Touch Rule** inside the shooting range boundary*.

STEP 7 - Scrimmage (Cooperative and Competitive)
- Apply the **One Touch Rule** inside the shooting range boundary*.

STEP 8 - Cool-Down
- Review the **shooting technique.**

STEP 9 - End of Practice
- Compliment each player's improvement in their **shooting technique!**

*See top of page 82 for an explanation of shooting range boundary.

Passing

OBJECTIVE: To realize and develop the habit of effective **'Passing'**.

STEP 1 - Begin Practice with Explanation and Demonstration

Passing between players is the invisible string that brings a team together. The most widely used technique used for this purpose is the Push or Cup of the shoe pass, which consists of:

HEAD:
Rock steady, with eyes on the ball.

UPPER BODY:
Upright.

ARMS:
Out for balance.

PASSING LEG:
Knee bent, pendulum type swing, toes to knee (locks ankle), follow through.

PLANTED FOOT:
Knee bent, pointing in direction of release.

Passing

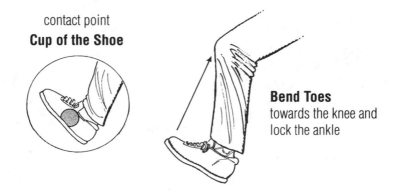

contact point
Cup of the Shoe

Bend Toes
towards the knee and
lock the ankle

The ball is also passed with:

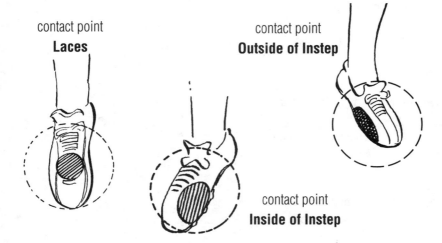

contact point
Laces

contact point
Outside of Instep

contact point
Inside of Instep

Common to all four passes:
- Relaxed "monkey stance". Both knees are slightly bent throughout the passing motion.
- Each pass begins with bringing the passing foot behind the plant foot using a pendulum type swing.
- The ankle is locked before contact with the ball.
- Always finish with the follow through.

Passing

STEP 2 - Warm-Up
- Use **Push-Peek-Push** sequence during Figure 8 Stretch Routine.
- **Push** ball using **cup of shoe** only.

Push Off

STEP 3 - ONE + ONE (Cooperative Time)
- Adjust "The SERVE" to practice (cup of shoe) passing.

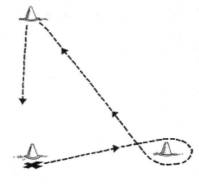

Receiver - Run through pattern and become cooperative passing target.

Server - Take ball through pattern with cup of shoe, pass hard to feet and soft to space.

LEFT FOOT ONLY

Screen

RIGHT FOOT ONLY

Pass

LEFT FOOT FAKE

Screen

Peek

Push

Pull

Passing

STEP 4 - ONE vs. ONE
- Begin every game with "The SERVE".
- "The SERVE" is adjusted and disguises the repetitious practice of the **passing** technique.

STEP 5 - Half-Time Routine
- Water and relax.
- Review Explanation/Demonstration of **passing.**

STEP 6 - Small Sided Games (Cooperative and Competitive)
- Enforce **Two-Touch Rule** during these games to focus on passing.

STEP 7 - Scrimmage (Cooperative and Competitive)
- Enforce **Two-Touch Rule** during these games to focus on passing.

STEP 8 - Cool-Down
- Review **passing** technique.

STEP 9 - End of Practice
- Compliment each player's improvement in **passing!**

Theme: Release the Ball

Throw-In

OBJECTIVE: To realize and develop the habit of the effective **'Throw-In'**.

STEP 1 - Begin Practice with Explanation and Demonstration

Laws of the Game (Law XV. – Throw-In)
When the whole of the ball passes over a touch-line, either on the ground or in the air, it shall be thrown in from the point where it crossed the line, in any direction, by a player of the team opposite to that of the player who last touched it. The thrower at the moment of delivering the ball must face the field of play and part of each foot shall be either on the touch-line or on the ground outside the touch-line. The thrower shall use both hands and shall deliver the ball from behind and over his head. The ball shall be in play immediately after it enters the field of play, but the thrower shall not again play the ball until it has been touched or played by another player. A goal shall not be scored direct from a throw-in.

Key Points:
1 - Part of each foot has to touch ground prior to release of the ball.
2 - The ball delivery must originate from behind the head and be thrown over it.
3 - The ball must be thrown, not dropped.
4 - Both hands must be used simultaneously or with equal force.
5 - The player must face the direction of the throw.

Throw-In

STEP 2 - Warm-Up
- Focus on the upper body
  muscles during Figure 8
  Stretch Routine.

STEP 3 - ONE + ONE (Cooperative Time)
- Adjust "The SERVE" to practice the proper
  throw-in technique.

STEP 4 - ONE vs. ONE
- Begin every game with "The SERVE".

STEP 5 - Half-Time Routine
- Water and relax.
- Review Explanation/Demonstration of the **throw-in.**

STEP 6 - Small Sided Games (Cooperative and Competitive)
- **Start all actions and infractions with a throw-in.**

STEP 7 - Scrimmage (Cooperative and Competitive)
- **Start all actions and infractions with a throw-in.**

STEP 8 - Cool-Down
- Review **throw-in** technique.

STEP 9 - End of Practice
- Compliment each player's improvement in **throw-in!**

Visit our website:
FUNdamentalsoccer.com
for exchanging attacking theme ideas!

FUNdamental Soccer

Soccer

Section 5

Defending Themes

Peeking

OBJECTIVE: To realize and develop the habit of the effective **'Peeking'** while defending.

STEP 1 - Begin Practice with Explanation and Demonstration
- Introduce the phrase: "Ball in flight - **peek** left and right".
- Anytime the ball is traveling between players, **peek** to see:
- Where is the goal to defend?
- Where is the ball.
- Where is the most dangerous attacker?
- Where are my teammates?

STEP 2 - Warm-Up
- Practice **peeking** during the Figure 8 Stretch Routine.
- First attacker dribbling forward and first defender practices **peeking.**

*Teach them as first defender **'Eyes down on the ball, watch the ball - that is all!'***

Peeking

STEP 3 - ONE + ONE (Cooperative Time)
- "The SERVE" compels practice of the **peeking** technique.
- Instructions given to both players. They are to **peek** left and right and take their eyes off the ball when the ball is travelling between them.

STEP 4 - ONE vs. ONE
- Begin every game with "The SERVE".
- "The SERVE" provides an ideal setting for disguising the repetitious practice of the **peeking** technique.

STEP 5 - Half-Time Routine
- Water and relax.
- Review Explanation/Demonstration of **peeking.**

STEP 6 - Small Sided Games (Cooperative and Competitive)
- Teach and encourage defensive **peeking.**

STEP 7 - Scrimmage (Cooperative and Competitive)
- Teach and encourage defensive **peeking.**

STEP 8 - Cool-Down
- Review **peeking** technique

STEP 9 - End of Practice
- Compliment each player's improvement in **peeking!**

Moving

OBJECTIVE: To realize and develop the habit of the effective **'Moving'** while defending.

STEP 1 - Begin Practice with Explanation and Demonstration
- Coach them how to **move:**
- First, into a position to block their goal.
- Then, to go and pressure the ball.

- Coach them how to **move** to prevent first attacker from:
- Moving forward, passing, crossing, shooting or scoring.
- Seeing either the attacking goal or teammates.

Teach them as first defender:

| *First, into a position to block the goal.* | *Then, to go and pressure the ball.* |

STEP 2 - Warm-Up
- Practice **moving** in the defensive stance during the Figure 8 Stretch Routine.
- Moving forwards, backwards, shuffling, foot faking and body feinting!

STEP 3 - ONE + ONE (Cooperative Time)
- After "The SERVE" practice proper defensive **moving.**

Moving

STEP 4 - ONE vs. ONE
- Begin every game with "The SERVE".
- "The SERVE" is adjusted and disguises the repetitious practice of proper defensive **moving.**

STEP 5 - Half-Time Routine
- Water and relax.
- Review Explanation/Demonstration of **moving.**

STEP 6 - Small Sided Games (Cooperative and Competitive)
- Teach and encourage **moving** to block the goal and then pressure the ball.

STEP 7 - Scrimmage (Cooperative and Competitive)
- Teach and encourage **moving** to block the goal and then pressure the ball.

STEP 8 - Cool-Down
- Review **moving** technique.

STEP 9 - End of Practice
- Compliment each player's improvement in **moving!**

Ready Stance

OBJECTIVE: To realize and develop the habit of the effective **'Ready Stance'**.

STEP 1 - Begin Practice with Explanation and Demonstration
All Defensive moves are initiated from the 'Ready Stance'. This position should be instinctively assumed whenever the opponent gains possession of the ball.

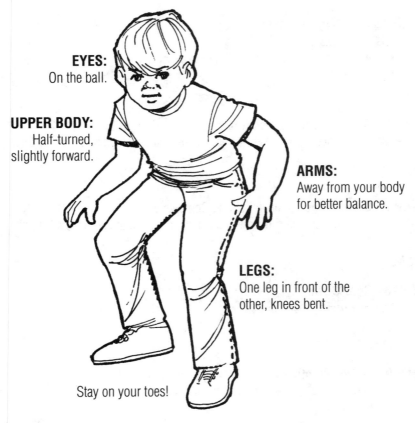

EYES:
On the ball.

UPPER BODY:
Half-turned,
slightly forward.

ARMS:
Away from your body
for better balance.

LEGS:
One leg in front of the
other, knees bent.

Stay on your toes!

This position is similar to that taken by a basketball player or boxer.

Important: Be balanced by playing on the balls of the feet not flatfooted. Be mentally alert and ready to move in any direction.

Ready Stance

STEP 1 - Explanation and Demonstration

Time to run quickly is while ball is traveling to your opponent.

*If interception is not possible slow down run by dropping buttocks (bending knees) and gliding into **Ready Stance** keeping both feet moving.*	*Get within 'striking' distance of First Attacker. Ideally two yards from the ball.*

Overplay the First Attacker - that is, play off his shoulder to make play predictable in one direction.	*Nose even with First Attacker's shoulder.*

Ready Stance

STEP 2 - Warm-Up
- Practice **ready stance moving** in the Figure 8 Stretch Routine.
- Moving forwards, backwards, and sideways!

Push Off

STEP 3 - ONE + ONE (Cooperative Time)
- After "The SERVE" **ready stance** practice begins.

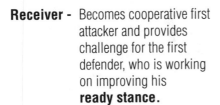

Receiver - Becomes cooperative first attacker and provides challenge for the first defender, who is working on improving his **ready stance.**

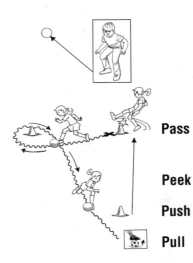

Pass

Server - Practices **ready stance** vs. cooperative first attacker.

Peek

Push

Pull

Ready Stance

STEP 4 - ONE vs. ONE
- Begin every game with "The SERVE".
- "The SERVE" is adjusted and disguises the repetitious practice of the **ready stance.**

STEP 5 - Half-Time Routine
- Water and relax.
- Review Explanation/Demonstration of the **ready stance.**

STEP 6 - Small Sided Games (Cooperative and Competitive)
- Teach and encourage using the **ready stance.**

STEP 7 - Scrimmage (Cooperative and Competitive)
- Teach and encourage using the **ready stance.**

STEP 8 - Cool-Down
- Review **ready stance** technique.

STEP 9 - End of Practice
- Compliment each player's improvement in **ready stance!**

Poking

OBJECTIVE: To realize and develop the habit of effective '**Poking**' while defending.

STEP 1 - Begin Practice with Explanation and Demonstration

Keep the first attacker under control by forcing him to watch the ball. Make the first attacker play defensively, that is protecting the ball from you. This is accomplished by **poking** at the ball in the following manner:

EYES:
On the ball.

UPPER BODY:
Half-turned,
slightly forward.

ARMS:
Away from your
body for better
balance.

**FRONT FOOT
(POKER):**
Fakes and makes
attempts at the ball.

**BACK FOOT
(PLANTER):**
Bend the knee.

Poking

STEP 1 - Explanation and Demonstration

Back foot supports the body
weight.

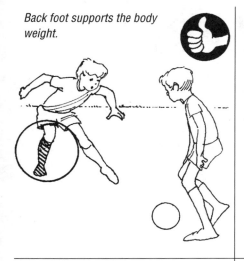

Front foot 'Poker' makes attempts
to gain possession of the ball.

Keep eyes on the ball. Avoid watching
feet/body for a fake may fool you.

Shuffle feet and avoid crossing them.

Most Important: Keep your body between the goal and the ball.

Poking

STEP 2 - Warm-Up
- Practice **poking** during the Figure 8 Stretch Routine.

STEP 3 - ONE + ONE (Cooperative Time)
- After "The SERVE" **poking** practice begins.

Push Off

Receiver - Becomes first attacker and dribbles at appropriate speed, so first defender can work on the **poking** techinque.

Server - Becomes first defender and practices **poking** vs. cooperative first attacker.

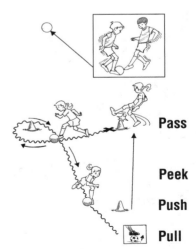

Pass

Peek

Push

Pull

Poking

STEP 4 - ONE vs. ONE
- Begin every game with "The SERVE".
- Players experiment using the **poking** technique after "The SERVE".

STEP 5 - Half-Time Routine
- Water and relax.
- Review Explanation/Demonstration of **poking.**

STEP 6 - Small Sided Games (Cooperative and Competitive)
- Teach and encourage **poking.**

STEP 7 - Scrimmage (Cooperative and Competitive)
- Teach and encourage **poking.**

STEP 8 - Cool-Down
- Review **poking** technique

STEP 9 - End of Practice
- Compliment each player's improvement in **poking!**

Block Tackling

OBJECTIVE: To realize and develop the habit of the effective **'Block Tackling'**.

STEP 1 - Begin Practice with Explanation and Demonstration
- When assured of having teammate behind to cover.
- First defender uses movement similar to a strong inside-of-the-foot pass, at the moment of impact with the ball:

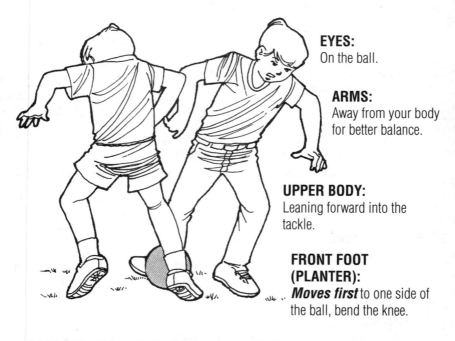

EYES:
On the ball.

ARMS:
Away from your body for better balance.

UPPER BODY:
Leaning forward into the tackle.

FRONT FOOT (PLANTER):
Moves first to one side of the ball, bend the knee.

BACK FOOT (TACKLER): *Moves second* to the middle of the ball, bend knee slightly, flex toes toward knee to keep ankle tight. Meet power with power!

Block Tackling

STEP 1 - Explanation and Demonstration

Contact middle of ball.

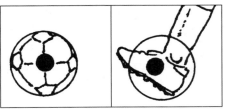

Contact the ball with "cup" of shoe.

Raise 'cup' after contact to roll ball over 1st Attacker's shoe.

> **Important:** Do not lunge at the ball. Realize that you will not always win the ball. Be satisfied to occasionally poke or kick the ball away.

Block Tackling

STEP 2 - Warm-Up
- Practice **block tackling** during the Figure 8 Stretch Routine.

Push Off

STEP 3 - ONE + ONE (Cooperative Time)
- After "The SERVE" **block tackling** practice begins.

Receiver - Becomes first attacker and dribbles at appropriate speed so first defender can work on the **block tackling** techinque.

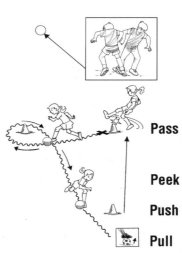

Pass

Peek

Push

Pull

Server - Becomes first defender and practices **block tackling** vs. cooperative first attacker.

Block Tackling

STEP 4 - ONE vs. ONE
- Begin every game with "The SERVE".
- Players experiment using the **block tackling** technique after "The SERVE".

STEP 5 - Half-Time Routine
- Water and relax.
- Review Explanation/Demonstration of **block tackling.**

STEP 6 - Small Sided Games (Cooperative and Competitive)
- Teach and encourage **block tackling.**

STEP 7 - Scrimmage (Cooperative and Competitive)
- Teach and encourage **block tackling.**

STEP 8 - Cool-Down
- Review **block tackling** technique

STEP 9 - End of Practice
- Compliment each player's improvement in **block tackling!**

Notes for Better Coaching

- Consistent-sequential exposure to the 'FUNdamental practice routine' will produce real results.

- A practice session is rehearsal for the game day routine. Duplicate the excitement of the game in your practices.

- The genius of good coaching is to make hard work seem like FUN. Players will continue to participate if they are having FUN.

- When player and ball are moving, learning is taking place. When player or ball stop moving, learning stops!

- Allow them to experiment and play their way to success! Permit the players to make mistakes and learn from them.

- Learning takes place, resulting from errors made, if the player is instructed correctly both verbally and physically.

MAKE IT WORK • MAKE IT BETTER • INTRODUCE OPPOSITION
A. Maher

REMEMBER: Everything takes time to learn.

Final Notes for Better Coaching

- Encourage questions and discussion.

- Encourage the players when appropriate.

- You must take a players' mistake, a negative experience and turn it into a positive situation.

- Try to improve one technique at each practice session. Provide only one tip or suggestion on improvement at a time.

- Prepare them for the unexpected in the game. Create an atmosphere where players are teaching themselves!

- Let the players be creative!

- Be patient, learning occurs slowly and that is why patience is not only a virtue, but a coaching necessity!

- Teach the players correctly and they will learn the correct way.

- Teach them at practice what they can work on at home (hint: 1 vs. 1 game).
  Teach them at practice what they must work on at home (hint: 1 vs. 1 game).

VERY FINAL NOTE:
The outcome of our children is infinitely more important than the outcome of any practice/game you will ever coach.

FUNdamental SOCCER – GUIDE

Using a maximum number of clever illustrations and a minimum number of words, this 111 page book GUIDES you into the world of youth soccer. Receive detailed information on the role of the participants: Players; Officials; Coach; Manager and Parents. Both attacking and defending techniques as well as the Laws of the Game are thoroughly covered. This is a must read book for anyone involved in youth soccer.

FUNdamental SOCCER – TACTICS

Was written to assist youth coaches in prior planning and organizing practices, which will prevent poor game performance. The illustrations, together with brief instructions, simplify the teaching of soccer tactics. Receive FUNdamental action plans for successful attacking and defending in this 128 page book. Recommended, "Modified Laws of the Game" for U-6, U-8, and U-10 age groups are also included.

FUNdamental SOCCER – GOALKEEPING

The "kick-off" to becoming a successful goalkeeper! This book offers tips to youth players and coaches on technique development for this specialized position. Dr. Joseph Machnik, former US National team goalkeeper coach said, "I loved it!...the book fulfills the needs of very young goalkeepers and their coaches by emphasizing the positive aspects of the position and the enjoyment which comes through efforts to perform properly as a goalkeeper." This 128 page book is full of descriptive illustrations with down-to-earth instructions.

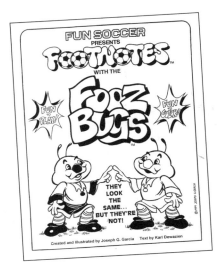

FOOZ BUGS

They look the same...But they're not!

There are 10 differences between the top and bottom cartoons. Can you and your players find them? That is the challenge of this combination coloring, tease and test booklet which was designed to bring Mom, Dad and player to the sport of soccer. This family activity booklet gives Mom & Dad an opportunity to introduce and discuss, in a FUNdamental way, the 'Laws of the Game'.

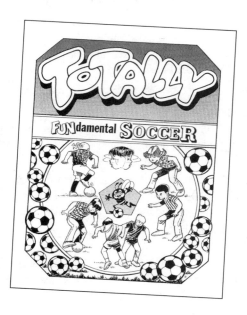

TOTALLY – FUNdamental Soccer

Is the players supplement to the "FUNdamental - Practice" book. It supports the extremely successful training method introduced in the "Practice" book. This 70 page book is designed in a coloring book format and excites the players to 'want to' practice at home what has been taught in practice. Beginning with imagery and shadow training, the players are guided toward playing the 1 vs. 1 game at home. Also, every necessary First Attacker and Defender technique is detailed with the use of the proper 'buzz' words. This is a must 'read/color/study' book for all young players…!

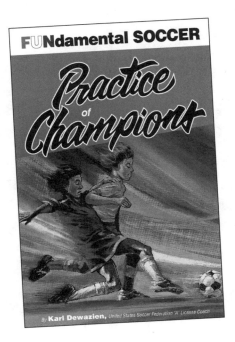

**FUNdamental Soccer –
Practice of Champions is now on video.**

The 9 Step Practice Routine is also available on DVD!